This journal belongs to:

ME 💗

YOU 💗

ANNIVERSARIES	
WE MET	
OUR FIRST KISS	
WE COMMITTED TO EACH OTHER	

OUR LOVE STORY

A GUIDED JOURNAL TO LEARN MORE ABOUT EACH OTHER

chartwell
books

Contents

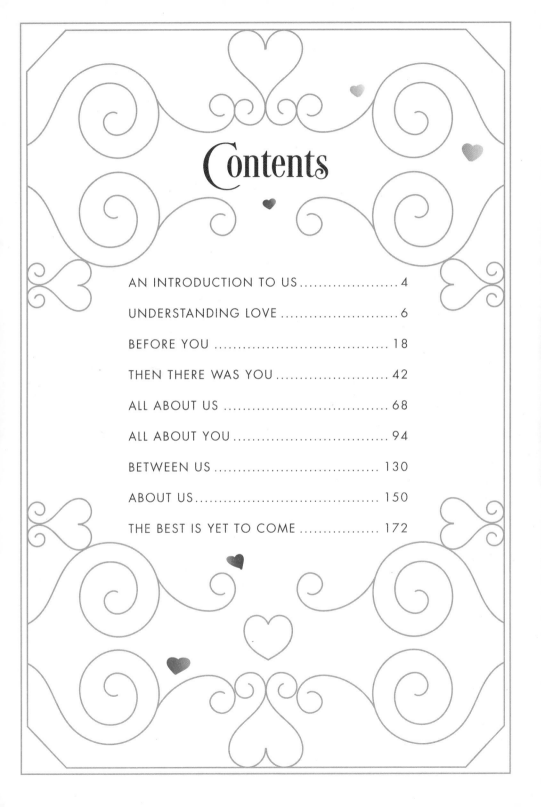

An Introduction to Us

There are countless reasons why it had to be you—why it had to be us—from our childhood dreams about the person we'd one day be with to all the twists and turns that brought us together. Incalculable forces brought us together, and now, nothing can keep us apart. This journal is the story of us—who we were, who we are, and who we hope to be one day. It will explore and celebrate our love, as we write about each other and our shared experiences.

How to Use This Journal

Each of us gets a different color heart—you get pink, I get violet.

When there's one heart on the page, the person with that color heart

writes on that page. When the hearts are joined, write together.

ME = ♥ ♥ = YOU

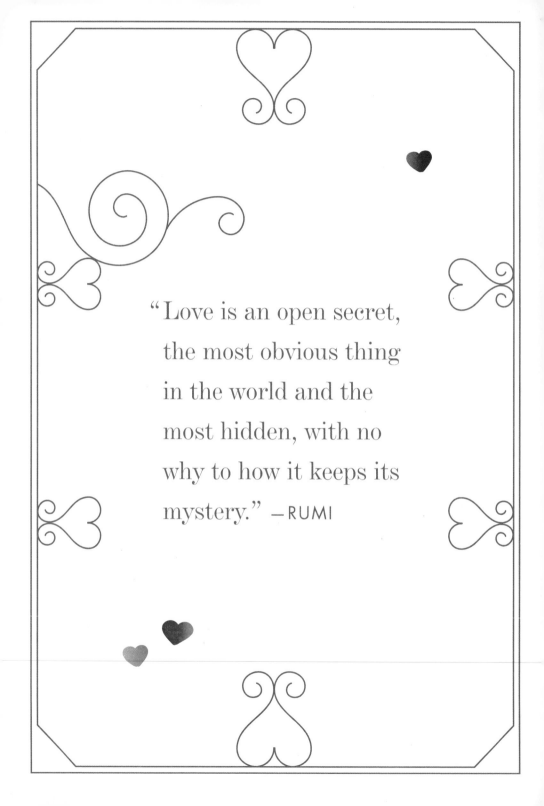

"Love is an open secret,
the most obvious thing
in the world and the
most hidden, with no
why to how it keeps its
mystery." —RUMI

UNDERSTANDING LOVE

Love is a word,

a feeling,

a world to live in.

But love is a language

we grow into.

Understanding love

has been a journey

that led me to you…

I GREW UP THINKING LOVE WAS ABOUT . . .

....
....
....
....
....
....
....
....
....
....
....
....
....
....
....
....
....
....
....
....
....
....
....
....
....
....

I GREW UP THINKING LOVE WAS ABOUT . . .

I DEFINE LOVE AS . . .

....
....
....
....
....
....
....
....
....
....
....
....

THE PURPOSE OF LOVE IS . . .

....
....
....
....
....
....
....
....
....
....
....
....
....
....

I DEFINE LOVE AS . . .

....
....
....
....
....
....
....
....
....
....
....
....

THE PURPOSE OF LOVE IS . . .

....
....
....
....
....
....
....
....
....
....
....
....
....
....
....
....

YOU TAUGHT ME LOVE WAS . . .

....
....
....
....
....
....
....
....
....
....
....

OUR LOVE IS BUILT ON . . .

....
....
....
....
....
....
....
....
....
....
....
....
....

♥

YOU TAUGHT ME LOVE WAS . . .

....
....
....
....
....
....
....
....
....
....
....
....
....

OUR LOVE IS BUILT ON . . .

....
....
....
....
....
....
....
....
....
....
....
....
....
....

A MOMENT IN MY LIFE I WISH YOU WERE BY MY SIDE WAS . . .

A MOMENT IN MY LIFE I WISH YOU WERE BY MY SIDE WAS . . .

I Believe ...

In fate.	YES	NO
In love at first sight.	YES	NO
Opposites attract.	YES	NO
In soul mates.	YES	NO
Love conquers all.	YES	NO
You have to love yourself in order to be loved.	YES	NO
Love is infinite.	YES	NO

I Believe...

In fate.	YES	NO
In love at first sight.	YES	NO
Opposites attract.	YES	NO
In soul mates.	YES	NO
Love conquers all.	YES	NO
You have to love yourself in order to be loved.	YES	NO
Love is infinite.	YES	NO

"Love can only be
found through the
act of loving."

—PAULO COELHO

BEFORE YOU

Once upon a time we were children. We had lives separate from each other, as hard as that is to imagine now. The paths we were on turned us into the people we are today—and converged to bring us together. But before you…

WHEN I WAS A KID, I IMAGINED MY TRUE LOVE WOULD BE . . .

WHEN I WAS A KID, I IMAGINED MY TRUE LOVE WOULD BE . . .

I KNEW I WOULD END UP WITH SOMEONE LIKE YOU, WHO . . .

....
....
....
....
....
....
....
....
....
....
....

I NEVER THOUGHT I WOULD END UP WITH SOMEONE LIKE YOU, WHO . . .

....
....
....
....
....
....
....
....
....
....
....
....
....

♥

I KNEW I WOULD END UP WITH SOMEONE LIKE YOU, WHO . . .

....

....

....

....

....

....

....

....

....

....

....

....

I NEVER THOUGHT I WOULD END UP WITH SOMEONE LIKE YOU, WHO . . .

....

....

....

....

....

....

....

....

....

....

....

....

....

♥

IF THIS HAPPENED, WE WOULD HAVE NEVER MET . . .

....
....
....
....
....
....
....
....
....
....
....
....

BEFORE WE MET, I WAS SURE THAT . . .

....
....
....
....
....
....
....
....
....
....
....
....
....
....
....

♥

IF THIS HAPPENED, WE WOULD HAVE NEVER MET . . .

....

....

....

....

....

....

....

....

....

....

....

....

BEFORE WE MET, I WAS SURE THAT . . .

....

....

....

....

....

....

....

....

....

....

....

....

....

....

....

WRITE A LOVE POEM FOR YOUR PARTNER.

WRITE A LOVE POEM FOR YOUR PARTNER.

MY FAVORITE THING ABOUT BEING SINGLE WAS . . .

....
....
....
....
....
....
....
....
....
....
....
....
....

MY LEAST FAVORITE THING ABOUT BEING SINGLE WAS . . .

....
....
....
....
....
....
....
....
....
....
....
....
....

MY FAVORITE THING ABOUT BEING SINGLE WAS . . .

....
....
....
....
....
....
....
....
....
....
....
....
....

MY LEAST FAVORITE THING ABOUT BEING SINGLE WAS . . .

....
....
....
....
....
....
....
....
....
....
....
....
....
....

RIGHT BEFORE WE MET, I WAS . . .

....
....
....
....
....
....
....
....
....
....
....
....
....
....
....
....
....
....
....
....
....
....
....
....
....

RIGHT BEFORE WE MET, I WAS . . .

♥

THE GREATEST LESSON I LEARNED FROM YOU . . .

....
....
....
....
....
....
....
....
....
....
....
....
....

THE ONE THING I WISH I COULD DO FOR YOU . . .

....
....
....
....
....
....
....
....
....
....
....
....
....

THE GREATEST LESSON I LEARNED FROM YOU . . .

....
....
....
....
....
....
....
....
....
....
....
....
....

THE ONE THING I WISH I COULD DO FOR YOU . . .

....
....
....
....
....
....
....
....
....
....
....
....
....
....

I WILL ALWAYS FORGIVE YOU FOR . . .

....
....
....
....
....
....
....
....
....
....
....
....

OUR SECRET FOR SUCCESS IS . . .

....
....
....
....
....
....
....
....
....
....
....
....
....
....

I WILL ALWAYS FORGIVE YOU FOR . . .

....

....

....

....

....

....

....

....

....

....

....

....

....

OUR SECRET FOR SUCCESS IS . . .

....

....

....

....

....

....

....

....

....

....

....

....

....

....

....

WE WILL NEVER . . .

....
....
....
....
....
....
....
....
....
....
....
....
....

WE WILL ALWAYS . . .

....
....
....
....
....
....
....
....
....
....
....
....
....
....
....

WE WILL NEVER . . .

....
....
....
....
....
....
....
....
....
....
....
....
....

WE WILL ALWAYS . . .

....
....
....
....
....
....
....
....
....
....
....
....
....
....
....
....

PLAN YOUR NEXT DATE:

Look through the list of fun things to do together
and rate them individually. After you're both done,
see what'll be your next date!

OUR NEXT DATE NIGHT:

WATCH A TV SHOW/MOVIE TOGETHER.

(NOT INTERESTED)   1   2   3   4   5   (I'M INTO IT!)

EXERCISE TOGETHER.

(NOT INTERESTED)   1   2   3   4   5   (I'M INTO IT!)

COOK TOGETHER.

(NOT INTERESTED)   1   2   3   4   5   (I'M INTO IT!)

START A GARDEN TOGETHER.

(NOT INTERESTED)   1   2   3   4   5   (I'M INTO IT!)

BUILD SOMETHING TOGETHER.

(NOT INTERESTED)   1   2   3   4   5   (I'M INTO IT!)

TAKE A CLASS FOR SOMETHING NEW.

(NOT INTERESTED)   1   2   3   4   5   (I'M INTO IT!)

GO TO AN ARCADE/BOWLING ALLEY.

(NOT INTERESTED)   1   2   3   4   5   (I'M INTO IT!)

TRY NEW FOOD TOGETHER.

(NOT INTERESTED)   1   2   3   4   5   (I'M INTO IT!)

GO TO A FLEA MARKET TOGETHER.

(NOT INTERESTED)   1   2   3   4   5   (I'M INTO IT!)

TAKE A ROAD TRIP.

(NOT INTERESTED)   1   2   3   4   5   (I'M INTO IT!)

PLAN YOUR NEXT DATE:

Look through the list of fun things to do together and rate them individually. After you're both done, see what'll be your next date!

WATCH A TV SHOW/MOVIE TOGETHER.

(NOT INTERESTED)　　1　2　3　4　5　　(I'M INTO IT!)

EXERCISE TOGETHER.

(NOT INTERESTED)　　1　2　3　4　5　　(I'M INTO IT!)

COOK TOGETHER.

(NOT INTERESTED)　　1　2　3　4　5　　(I'M INTO IT!)

START A GARDEN TOGETHER.

(NOT INTERESTED)　　1　2　3　4　5　　(I'M INTO IT!)

BUILD SOMETHING TOGETHER.

(NOT INTERESTED)　　1　2　3　4　5　　(I'M INTO IT!)

TAKE A CLASS FOR SOMETHING NEW.

(NOT INTERESTED)　　1　2　3　4　5　　(I'M INTO IT!)

GO TO AN ARCADE/BOWLING ALLEY.

(NOT INTERESTED)　　1　2　3　4　5　　(I'M INTO IT!)

TRY NEW FOOD TOGETHER.

(NOT INTERESTED)　　1　2　3　4　5　　(I'M INTO IT!)

GO TO A FLEA MARKET TOGETHER.

(NOT INTERESTED)　　1　2　3　4　5　　(I'M INTO IT!)

TAKE A ROAD TRIP.

(NOT INTERESTED)　　1　2　3　4　5　　(I'M INTO IT!)

"They gave each other a smile with a future in it." —RING LARDNER

THEN THERE WAS YOU

When we met, a new chapter in our lives began. We were starting on a path to something big, something amazing, something that would last our lifetimes. I was once alone, but then there was you...

WE MET WHEN . . .

WE MET WHEN . . .

THE VERY FIRST TIME I SAW YOU, I THOUGHT . . .

THE VERY FIRST TIME I SAW YOU, I THOUGHT . . .

....
....
....
....
....
....
....
....
....
....
....
....
....
....
....
....
....
....
....
....
....
....
....
....
....
....

Draw a picture from early in your relationship.

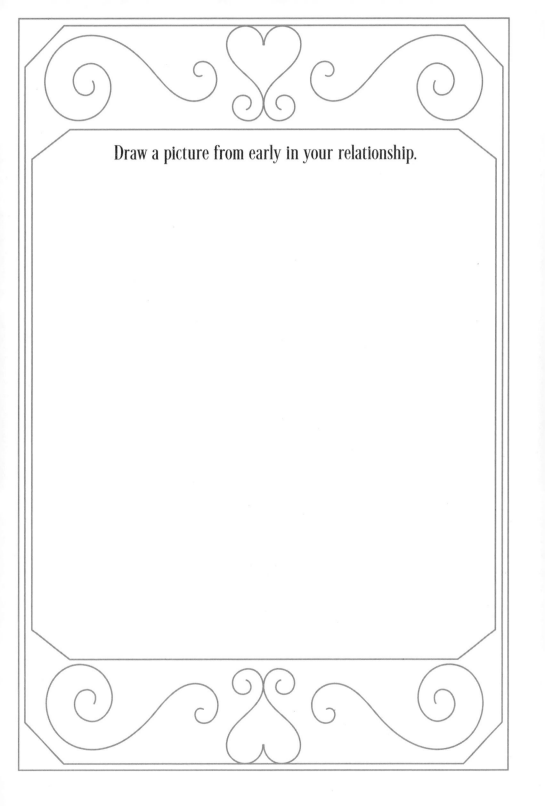

Draw a picture from early in your relationship.

OUR FIRST DATE WAS . . .

....

....

....

....

....

....

....

....

....

....

....

....

THE BEST PART OF THE DATE WAS . . .

....

....

....

....

....

....

....

....

....

....

....

....

....

....

OUR FIRST DATE WAS . . .

....
....
....
....
....
....
....
....
....
....
....
....

THE BEST PART OF THE DATE WAS . . .

....
....
....
....
....
....
....
....
....
....
....
....
....
....
....

AFTER OUR FIRST DATE, I THOUGHT . . .

....
....
....
....
....
....
....
....
....
....
....
....
....
....
....
....
....
....
....
....
....
....
....
....
....
....

♥

AFTER OUR FIRST DATE, I THOUGHT . . .

....

....

....

....

....

....

....

....

....

....

....

....

....

....

....

....

....

....

....

....

....

....

....

....

....

....

....

♥

IF I COULD GO BACK IN TIME AND GIVE MYSELF ADVICE BEFORE OUR
FIRST DATE, I WOULD TELL MYSELF . . .

....
....
....
....
....
....
....
....
....
....
....
....

IF I COULD GO BACK IN TIME AND GIVE YOU ADVICE BEFORE OUR
FIRST DATE, I WOULD TELL YOU . . .

....
....
....
....
....
....
....
....
....
....
....
....
....

IF I COULD GO BACK IN TIME AND GIVE MYSELF ADVICE BEFORE OUR
FIRST DATE, I WOULD TELL MYSELF . . .

....

....

....

....

....

....

....

....

....

....

....

....

IF I COULD GO BACK IN TIME AND GIVE YOU ADVICE BEFORE OUR
FIRST DATE, I WOULD TELL YOU . . .

....

....

....

....

....

....

....

....

....

....

....

....

....

WHEN WE FIRST STARTED DATING, I WAS SURE THAT . . .

WHEN WE FIRST STARTED DATING, I WAS SURE THAT . . .

DOODLING HEARTS WITH YOUR INITIALS IN THEM IS A CLASSIC WAY TO SAY
"I LOVE YOU." DOODLE SOME MESSAGES FOR EACH OTHER HERE.

Doodle Your Hearts Out

DOODLING HEARTS WITH YOUR INITIALS IN THEM IS A CLASSIC WAY TO SAY "I LOVE YOU." DOODLE SOME MESSAGES FOR EACH OTHER HERE.

Doodle Your Hearts Out

I KNEW I COULD TRUST YOU WHEN . . .

....
....
....
....
....
....
....
....
....
....
....
....
....

YOU TAUGHT ME WHAT LOVE WAS BY . . .

....
....
....
....
....
....
....
....
....
....
....
....
....
....
....

I KNEW I COULD TRUST YOU WHEN . . .

....

....

....

....

....

....

....

....

....

....

....

....

YOU TAUGHT ME WHAT LOVE WAS BY . . .

....

....

....

....

....

....

....

....

....

....

....

....

....

....

....

I KNEW I LOVED YOU WHEN . . .

....
....
....
....
....
....
....
....
....
....
....

I KNEW YOU LOVED ME WHEN . . .

....
....
....
....
....
....
....
....
....
....
....

I KNEW I LOVED YOU WHEN . . .

....

....

....

....

....

....

....

....

....

....

....

....

I KNEW YOU LOVED ME WHEN . . .

....

....

....

....

....

....

....

....

....

....

....

....

....

....

THE MOMENT I KNEW I COULDN'T LIVE WITHOUT YOU . . .

THE MOMENT I KNEW I COULDN'T LIVE WITHOUT YOU . . .

OUR LOVE STORY

FILL IN THE BLANKS WITH YOUR LOVE STORY.

It was a(n) _____ (ADJECTIVE), _____
(SEASON) afternoon when you _____ (VERB) by me and
said, "Hey."

My eyes _____ (VERB) as my heartbeat fluttered. In
that instant, I knew _____ (PARTNER'S NAME) and I would
love each other for _____ (LENGTH OF TIME). "Hey," I
said back. Then you looked deep into my _____
(NOUN) and replied, "_____" (INTERJECTION), you are
the _____ (SUPERLATIVE) girl / guy I have ever seen.
We sat in the _____ (PLACE) and stared at each other
for hours. We talked about _____ (NOUN) and other
important details of our lives. You loved _____
(NOUN) and _____ (NOUN) almost as much as I loved
_____ (NOUN). As your hand _____
(ADVERB) touched my _____ (NOUN), sparks flew.

I _____ (VERB) the way you _____
(VERB) me. We spent our time _____ (VERB+ING) in the
beginning. From then on we were never far apart. We have been
together ever since!

I am such a lucky _____ (NOUN) to have
_____ (NAME) in my _____ (NOUN)!

OUR LOVE STORY

FILL IN THE BLANKS WITH YOUR LOVE STORY.

It was a(n) _____ (ADJECTIVE), _____

(SEASON) afternoon when you _____ (VERB) by me and

said, "Hey."

My eyes _____ (VERB) as my heartbeat fluttered. In

that instant, I knew _____ (PARTNER'S NAME) and I would

love each other for _____ (LENGTH OF TIME). "Hey," I

said back. Then you looked deep into my _____

(NOUN) and replied, "_____" (INTERJECTION), you are

the _____ (SUPERLATIVE) girl / guy I have ever seen.

We sat in the _____ (PLACE) and stared at each other

for hours. We talked about _____ (NOUN) and other

important details of our lives. You loved _____

(NOUN) and _____ (NOUN) almost as much as I loved

_____ (NOUN). As your hand _____

(ADVERB) touched my _____ (NOUN), sparks flew.

I _____ (VERB) the way you _____

(VERB) me. We spent our time _____ (VERB+ING) in the

beginning. From then on we were never far apart. We have been

together ever since!

I am such a lucky _____ (NOUN) to have

_____ (NAME) in my _____ (NOUN)!

"Love does not consist in gazing at each other, but in looking together in the same direction."

—ANTOINE DE SAINT-EXUPÉRY

ALL ABOUT US

Our life together has been

an amazing adventure!

The ups are higher and

the downs are cushioned

because of our love.

Someone should write a

love story all about us…

OUR BEST DATE (SO FAR) WAS . . .

OUR FIRST BIG RELATIONSHIP STEP WAS . . .

THE FUNNIEST THING THAT HAS EVER HAPPENED TO US WAS . . .

THE HARDEST THING WE'VE BEEN THROUGH WAS . . .

OUR FIRST BIG FIGHT WAS . . .

WE MADE UP BY . . .

OUR BEST ANNIVERSARY SO FAR WAS . . .

OUR FAVORITE SONG:

♥

♥

OUR FAVORITE MOVIE:

♥

♥

OUR FAVORITE MEAL:

♥

♥

OUR FAVORITE PLACE:

♥

♥

OUR FAVORITE THING ABOUT US:

♥

♥

OUR FIRST TRIP TOGETHER WAS . . .

THE BEST MEAL WE'VE HAD WAS . . .

THINGS WE LIKE TO DO ON A QUIET NIGHT IN ARE . . .

WHEN WE WANT TO PAINT THE TOWN RED, WE . . .

THE BIGGEST THING WE HAVE IN COMMON IS . . .

THE BIGGEST DIFFERENCE BETWEEN US IS . . .

OUR RELATIONSHIP WORKS BECAUSE . . .

....
....
....
....
....
....
....
....
....
....
....
....
....

OUR BIGGEST STRENGTH AS A COUPLE IS . . .

....
....
....
....
....
....
....
....
....
....
....
....
....

OUR RELATIONSHIP WORKS BECAUSE . . .

....

....

....

....

....

....

....

....

....

....

....

....

OUR BIGGEST STRENGTH AS A COUPLE IS . . .

....

....

....

....

....

....

....

....

....

....

....

....

....

....

....

ONE THING WE COULD WORK ON IS . . .

....
....
....
....
....
....
....
....
....
....
....
....

WHEN WE'RE APART, I MISS . . .

....
....
....
....
....
....
....
....
....
....
....
....
....
....

ONE THING WE COULD WORK ON IS . . .

....
....
....
....
....
....
....
....
....
....
....
....

WHEN WE'RE APART, I MISS . . .

....
....
....
....
....
....
....
....
....
....
....
....
....
....

OUR LOVE LANGUAGES

Every person feels loved and appreciated in different ways. We each have our own language when it comes to love. Take a look at the 5 popular love languages. What language(s) do you and your loved one speak?

LOVE LANGUAGE	HOW LOVE IS COMMUNICATED . . .	ACTIONS I TAKE TO SHOW YOU YOUR LOVED:
WORDS OF AFFIRMATION	Feeling loved with appreciative, encouraging, and empathizing, comments.	1 _____ 2 _____
PHYSICAL TOUCH	Feeling loved through body language and touch like hugs, kisses, cuddling, and hand-holding.	3 _____
RECEIVING GIFTS	Feeling loved when your partner is thoughtful. They remember special occasions and do small things that show you that you matter.	**TO LISTEN BETTER, I WILL . . .** _____ _____ _____ _____
QUALITY TIME	Feeling loved with uninterrupted, one-on-one time used to create special moments together.	**I PROMISE TO . . .** _____ _____
ACTS OF SERVICE	Feeling loved when your partner is always ready to help and sharing responsibility.	_____ _____ _____

OUR LOVE LANGUAGES

Every person feels loved and appreciated in different ways. We each have our own language when it comes to love. Take a look at the 5 popular love languages. What language(s) do you and your loved one speak?

LOVE LANGUAGE	HOW LOVE IS COMMUNICATED . . .
WORDS OF AFFIRMATION	Feeling loved with appreciative, encouraging, and empathizing, comments.
PHYSICAL TOUCH	Feeling loved through body language and touch like hugs, kisses, cuddling, and hand-holding.
RECEIVING GIFTS	Feeling loved when your partner is thoughtful. They remember special occasions and do small things that show you that you matter.
QUALITY TIME	Feeling loved with uninterrupted, one-on-one time used to create special moments together.
ACTS OF SERVICE	Feeling loved when your partner is always ready to help and sharing responsibility.

ACTIONS I TAKE TO SHOW YOU YOUR LOVED:

1 _____

2 _____

3 _____

TO LISTEN BETTER, I WILL . . .

_____

_____

_____

_____

_____

I PROMISE TO . . .

_____

_____

_____

_____

_____

TO SHOW YOU I APPRECIATE YOU MORE, I WILL . . .

....
....
....
....
....
....
....
....
....
....
....

TO ENCOURAGE YOU, I WILL . . .

....
....
....
....
....
....
....
....
....
....
....
....
....
....

TO SHOW YOU I APPRECIATE YOU MORE, I WILL . . .

....
....
....
....
....
....
....
....
....
....
....
....
....

TO ENCOURAGE YOU, I WILL . . .

....
....
....
....
....
....
....
....
....
....
....
....
....

I WILL NEVER FORGET TO CELEBRATE OUR/YOUR . . .

....
....
....
....
....
....
....
....
....
....
....
....

I WILL MAKE TIME FOR US TO . . .

....
....
....
....
....
....
....
....
....
....
....
....
....
....

I WILL NEVER FORGET TO CELEBRATE OUR/YOUR . . .

....

....

....

....

....

....

....

....

....

....

....

I WILL MAKE TIME FOR US TO . . .

....

....

....

....

....

....

....

....

....

....

....

....

....

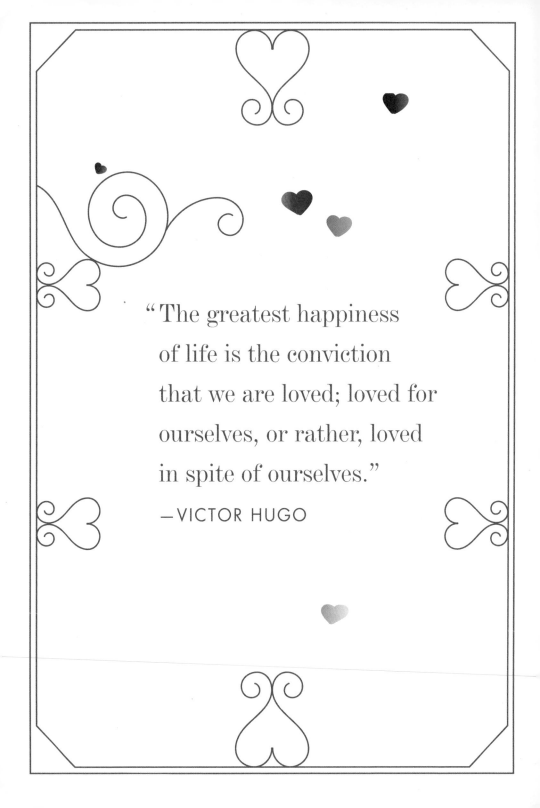

"The greatest happiness
of life is the conviction
that we are loved; loved for
ourselves, or rather, loved
in spite of ourselves."

—VICTOR HUGO

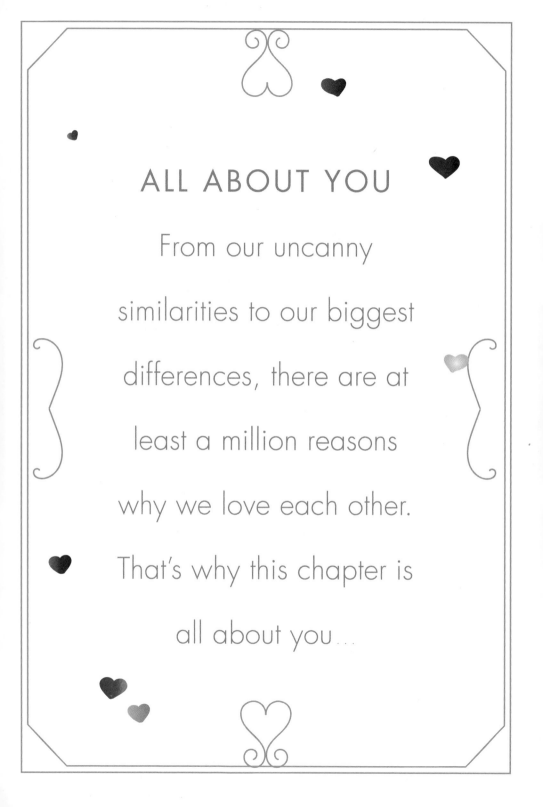

ALL ABOUT YOU

From our uncanny

similarities to our biggest

differences, there are at

least a million reasons

why we love each other.

That's why this chapter is

all about you...

MY FAVORITE THING THAT YOU DO IS . . .

....
....
....
....
....
....
....
....
....
....
....

I COULDN'T LIVE WITHOUT YOUR . . .

....
....
....
....
....
....
....
....
....
....
....
....
....
....
....

♥

MY FAVORITE THING THAT YOU DO IS . . .

....
....
....
....
....
....
....
....
....
....
....

I COULDN'T LIVE WITHOUT YOUR . . .

....
....
....
....
....
....
....
....
....
....
....
....
....
....
....

♥

I LOVE WHEN YOU . . .

....
....
....
....
....
....
....
....
....
....
....

YOU MAKE ME LAUGH WHEN YOU . . .

....
....
....
....
....
....
....
....
....
....
....
....

I LOVE WHEN YOU . . .

....
....
....
....
....
....
....
....
....
....
....

YOU MAKE ME LAUGH WHEN YOU . . .

....
....
....
....
....
....
....
....
....
....
....
....
....
....
....

THE STRANGEST THING YOU'VE EVER DONE IS . . .

....
....
....
....
....
....
....
....
....
....
....
....
....

THE ONLY TIME YOU SHOULD KEEP A SECRET IS WHEN . . .

....
....
....
....
....
....
....
....
....
....
....
....
....
....
....
....

THE STRANGEST THING YOU'VE EVER DONE IS . . .

....
....
....
....
....
....
....
....
....
....
....
....
....

THE ONLY TIME YOU SHOULD KEEP A SECRET IS WHEN . . .

....
....
....
....
....
....
....
....
....
....
....
....
....
....
....
....

THE THING THAT MAKES YOU UNIQUE IS . . .

....
....
....
....
....
....
....
....
....
....
....

YOUR TOP VALUES ARE . . .

....
....
....
....
....
....
....
....
....
....
....
....
....

THE THING THAT MAKES YOU UNIQUE IS . . .

....

....

....

....

....

....

....

....

....

....

....

....

YOUR TOP VALUES ARE . . .

....

....

....

....

....

....

....

....

....

....

....

....

....

....

Would You Rather?

RELATIONSHIPS ARE BUILT OVER TIME AND EVERYDAY WE LEARN SOMETHING NEW ABOUT EACH OTHER. I THINK I KNOW YOU PRETTY WELL! HERE ARE THE CHOICES I THINK YOU WOULD MAKE:

Drink coffee ♥ or ♥ Drink tea

Watch a movie ♥ or ♥ Go to a concert

Go on a cruise ♥ or ♥ Go camping

Live in the city ♥ or ♥ Live in the country

Walk on the beach ♥ or ♥ Go dancing

Watch a horror movie ♥ or ♥ Watch a comedy movie

Get up early ♥ or ♥ Sleep in late

Home-cooking ♥ or ♥ Take out

Eat savory ♥ or ♥ Eat sweet

Enjoy a gift ♥ or ♥ Want an experience

Go out ♥ or ♥ Stay in

Read a book ♥ or ♥ Watch a TV show

Drive ♥ or ♥ Be the passenger

Would You Rather?

RELATIONSHIPS ARE BUILT OVER TIME AND EVERYDAY WE LEARN SOMETHING NEW ABOUT EACH OTHER. I THINK I KNOW YOU PRETTY WELL! HERE ARE THE CHOICES I THINK YOU WOULD MAKE:

Drink coffee ♥ or ♥ Drink tea

Watch a movie ♥ or ♥ Go to a concert

Go on a cruise ♥ or ♥ Go camping

Live in the city ♥ or ♥ Live in the country

Walk on the beach ♥ or ♥ Go dancing

Watch a horror movie ♥ or ♥ Watch a comedy movie

Get up early ♥ or ♥ Sleep in late

Home-cooking ♥ or ♥ Take out

Eat savory ♥ or ♥ Eat sweet

Enjoy a gift ♥ or ♥ Want an experience

Go out ♥ or ♥ Stay in

Read a book ♥ or ♥ Watch a TV show

Drive ♥ or ♥ Be the passenger

I CAN'T GET ENOUGH OF YOUR . . .

....
....
....
....
....
....
....
....
....
....
....
....

THE BEST THING ABOUT YOU IS . . .

....
....
....
....
....
....
....
....
....
....
....
....
....
....

I CAN'T GET ENOUGH OF YOUR . . .

THE BEST THING ABOUT YOU IS . . .

YOUR FEEL ACCOMPLISHED WHEN. . .

....
....
....
....
....
....
....
....
....
....
....
....

YOUR PERFECT DAY INVOLVES. . .

....
....
....
....
....
....
....
....
....
....
....
....
....
....

YOUR FEEL ACCOMPLISHED WHEN. . .

YOUR PERFECT DAY INVOLVES. . .

YOU MAKE ME PROUD WHEN. . .

....

....

....

....

....

....

....

....

....

....

....

I ADORE YOU FOR. . .

....

....

....

....

....

....

....

....

....

....

....

....

YOU MAKE ME PROUD WHEN. . .

....

....

....

....

....

....

....

....

....

....

....

....

....

I ADORE YOU FOR. . .

....

....

....

....

....

....

....

....

....

....

....

....

....

....

....

IF YOU WERE A/AN. . .

Fill in the following statements with an answer that best describes your partner.

IF YOU WERE A FOOD, YOU'D BE

IF YOU WERE A SUPERHERO, YOU'D BE

IF YOU WERE AN ANIMAL, YOU'D BE

IF YOU WERE A PIECE OF CLOTHING, YOU'D BE

IF YOU WERE A SANDWICH, YOU'D BE

IF YOU WERE A COLOR, YOU'D BE

IF YOU WERE A BOOK, YOU'D BE

IF YOU WERE A MOVIE, YOU'D BE

IF YOU WERE A PLANT, YOU'D BE

IF YOU WERE A CHARACTER/CARTOON YOU'D BE

IF YOU WERE A/AN. . .

Fill in the following statements with an answer that best describes your partner.

IF YOU WERE A FOOD, YOU'D BE

IF YOU WERE A SUPERHERO, YOU'D BE

IF YOU WERE AN ANIMAL, YOU'D BE

IF YOU WERE A PIECE OF CLOTHING, YOU'D BE

IF YOU WERE A SANDWICH, YOU'D BE

IF YOU WERE A COLOR, YOU'D BE

IF YOU WERE A BOOK, YOU'D BE

IF YOU WERE A MOVIE, YOU'D BE

IF YOU WERE A PLANT, YOU'D BE

IF YOU WERE A CHARACTER/CARTOON YOU'D BE

MY FAVORITE PART OF YOUR BODY IS . . .

....
....
....
....
....
....
....
....
....
....
....
....

YOU GIVE ME GOOSEBUMPS WHEN . . .

....
....
....
....
....
....
....
....
....
....
....
....
....
....

MY FAVORITE PART OF YOUR BODY IS . . .

....

....

....

....

....

....

....

....

....

....

....

YOU GIVE ME GOOSEBUMPS WHEN . . .

....

....

....

....

....

....

....

....

....

....

....

....

....

....

YOU AMAZE ME WHEN . . .

....
....
....
....
....
....
....
....
....
....
....
....

YOU'VE INSPIRED ME TO . . .

....
....
....
....
....
....
....
....
....
....
....
....
....
....

YOU AMAZE ME WHEN . . .

....

....

....

....

....

....

....

....

....

....

....

....

YOU'VE INSPIRED ME TO . . .

....

....

....

....

....

....

....

....

....

....

....

....

....

....

I AM GRATEFUL FOR YOU BECAUSE . . .

....
....
....
....
....
....
....
....
....
....
....

YOU'RE THE BEST PARTNER BECAUSE . . .

....
....
....
....
....
....
....
....
....
....
....
....
....

I AM GRATEFUL FOR YOU BECAUSE . . .

YOU'RE THE BEST PARTNER BECAUSE . . .

YOU'VE MADE ME A BETTER PERSON BY . . .

....

....

....

....

....

....

....

....

....

....

....

....

I MISS YOU MOST WHEN . . .

....

....

....

....

....

....

....

....

....

....

....

....

....

....

YOU'VE MADE ME A BETTER PERSON BY . . .

I MISS YOU MOST WHEN . . .

FILL IN THE LOVE

When you_____, my heart beats faster.

Your eyes are _____. My favorite

quirk of yours is _____ I can never get

enough of your _____. Every time you

_____, I feel weak in the knees. I remember

when you told me _____. I hope you will

alway _____. Your _____is the

absolute best! My biggest wish for you is _____.

Every time you_____ , I am always impressed.

I laugh every time you _____. I love to watch

you _____. You remind me of the superhero

_____ because _____.

I wish I could _____ like you. You are my

_____ and my _____.

FILL IN THE LOVE

When you_____, my heart beats faster.

Your eyes are _____. My favorite

quirk of yours is _____ I can never get

enough of your _____. Every time you

_____, I feel weak in the knees. I remember

when you told me _____. I hope you will

alway _____. Your _____ is the

absolute best! My biggest wish for you is _____.

Every time you_____ , I am always impressed.

I laugh every time you _____. I love to watch

you _____. You remind me of the superhero

_____ because _____.

I wish I could _____ like you. You are my

_____ and my _____.

YOU SHOWED ME HOW TO . . .

....
....
....
....
....
....
....
....
....
....
....
....

YOU'RE MY HERO BECAUSE . . .

....
....
....
....
....
....
....
....
....
....
....
....
....
....

♥

YOU SHOWED ME HOW TO . . .

....

....

....

....

....

....

....

....

....

....

....

YOU'RE MY HERO BECAUSE . . .

....

....

....

....

....

....

....

....

....

....

....

....

....

....

YOU'VE TAUGHT ME TO . . .

....
....
....
....
....
....
....
....
....
....
....

YOU'VE TAUGHT ME TO . . .

....
....
....
....
....
....
....
....
....
....
....
....
....

YOU'VE TAUGHT ME TO . . .

YOU'VE TAUGHT ME TO . . .

I CAN NEVER THANK YOU ENOUGH FOR . . .

....
....
....
....
....
....
....
....
....
....
....
....

I CAN ALWAYS COUNT ON YOU TO . . .

....
....
....
....
....
....
....
....
....
....
....
....
....
....

I CAN NEVER THANK YOU ENOUGH FOR . . .

....
....
....
....
....
....
....
....
....
....
....

I CAN ALWAYS COUNT ON YOU TO . . .

....
....
....
....
....
....
....
....
....
....
....
....
....
....

"I love you and I like you."

—LESLIE KNOPE, *PARKS AND RECREATION*

BETWEEN US

We share so many deep

secrets, inside jokes,

daily habits, and little

rituals that make our lives

together rich and full of

love. But all that stuff is

just between us...

THE CUTEST THING YOU DO THAT ONLY I KNOW ABOUT IS . . .

....
....
....
....
....
....
....
....
....
....
....

I WOULD NEVER TELL ANYONE BUT YOU THAT . . .

....
....
....
....
....
....
....
....
....
....
....
....
....

THE CUTEST THING YOU DO THAT ONLY I KNOW ABOUT IS . . .

....
....
....
....
....
....
....
....
....
....
....
....

I WOULD NEVER TELL ANYONE BUT YOU THAT . . .

....
....
....
....
....
....
....
....
....
....
....
....
....
....

OUR BEST INSIDE JOKES ARE . . .

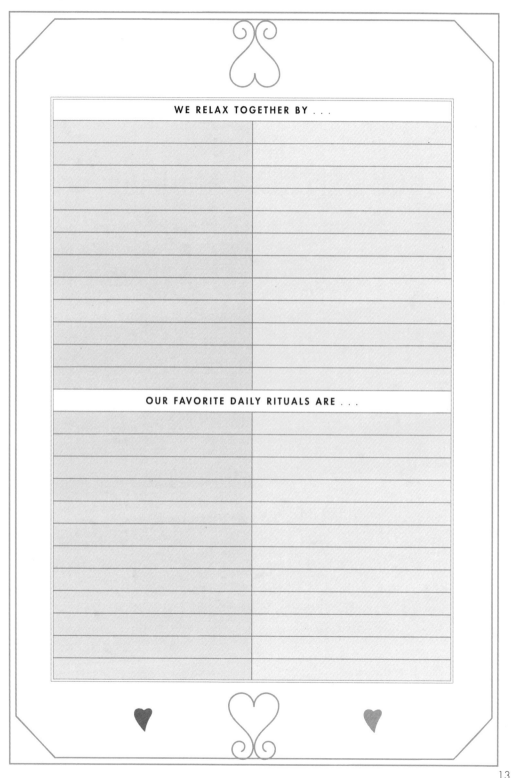

WE RELAX TOGETHER BY . . .

OUR FAVORITE DAILY RITUALS ARE . . .

OUR SECRET LANGUAGE

WE KNOW EACH OTHER SO WELL, WE CAN
COMMUNICATE BY JUST A LOOK OR CODE WORD THAT
ONLY WE UNDERSTAND. HERE'S OUR CODEBOOK:

♥♥ I love you! _____

♥♥ You are so adorable! _____

♥♥ I want you! _____

♥♥ You are hilarious! _____

♥♥ I completely agree. _____

♥♥ Relax; there's nothing we can do about it. _____

♥♥ Be careful with what you say next. _____

♥♥ I'm fine. _____

♥♥ Save me! _____

♥♥ I need some reassurance. _____

♥♥ You're my favorite person ever. _____

♥♥ Let's get out of here soon. _____

♥♥ We're leaving right now. _____

♥♥ I can't believe this is happening! _____

♥♥ I'm starving! _____

♥♥ You can eat the last one. _____

♥♥ ou better not eat the last one! _____

♥♥ Let's buy this one. _____

♥♥ Let's not get anything at this place. _____

♥♥ Can you believe this guy/gal?! _____

♥♥ I need help with this. _____

♥♥ Let's go help that person. _____

♥♥ Let's avoid that person. _____

OUR RELATIONSHIP WAS NEVER ABOUT . . .

OUR LOVE IS BUILT ON . . .

I SHOW MY LOVE BY . . .

....
....
....
....
....
....
....
....
....
....
....

I FEEL LOVED WHEN . . .

....
....
....
....
....
....
....
....
....
....
....
....
....
....
....

♥

I SHOW MY LOVE BY . . .

....

....

....

....

....

....

....

....

....

....

I FEEL LOVED WHEN . . .

....

....

....

....

....

....

....

....

....

....

....

....

....

WE OVERCOME OBSTACLES BY . . .

....
....
....
....
....
....
....
....
....
....
....
....
....
....
....
....
....
....
....
....
....
....
....
....
....
....
....

WE OVERCOME OBSTACLES BY . . .

OUR BEST CONVERSATIONS ARE USUALLY ABOUT . . .

OUR FAVORITE THINGS TO DO WHEN IT'S JUST US ARE . . .

WE REALLY GET EACH OTHER WHEN IT COMES TO . . .

THE MOST SPECIAL, PRIVATE MOMENT WE'VE SHARED IS . . .

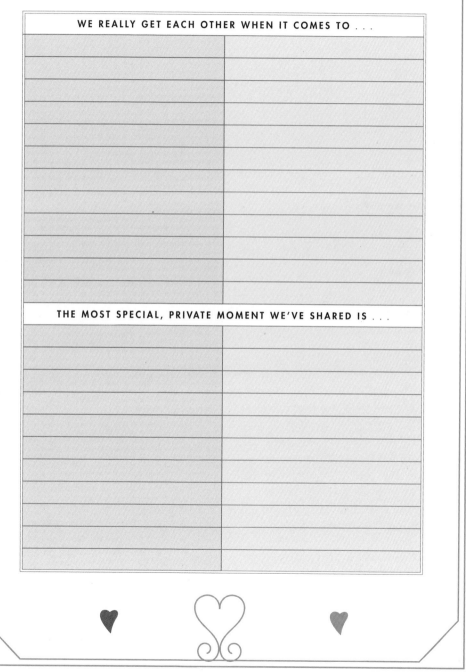

IF YOU HAD TO DESCRIBE ME, YOU'D SAY. . .

THE QUALITIES YOU BRING TO OUR RELATIONSHIP ARE. . .

IF YOU HAD TO DESCRIBE ME, YOU'D SAY. . .

....

....

....

....

....

....

....

....

....

....

THE QUALITIES YOU BRING TO OUR RELATIONSHIP ARE. . .

....

....

....

....

....

....

....

....

....

....

....

....

....

....

RELATIONSHIP WIT & WISDOM

- Never go to bed angry.
- Only when the right person comes along can you finally see why all the others were wrong.
- Absence makes the heart grow fonder.
- You can't rush something that you want to last forever.

MY OWN WIT & WISDOM

RELATIONSHIP WIT & WISDOM

- Never go to bed angry.
- Only when the right person comes along can you finally see why all the others were wrong.
- Absence makes the heart grow fonder.
- You can't rush something that you want to last forever.

MY OWN WIT & WISDOM

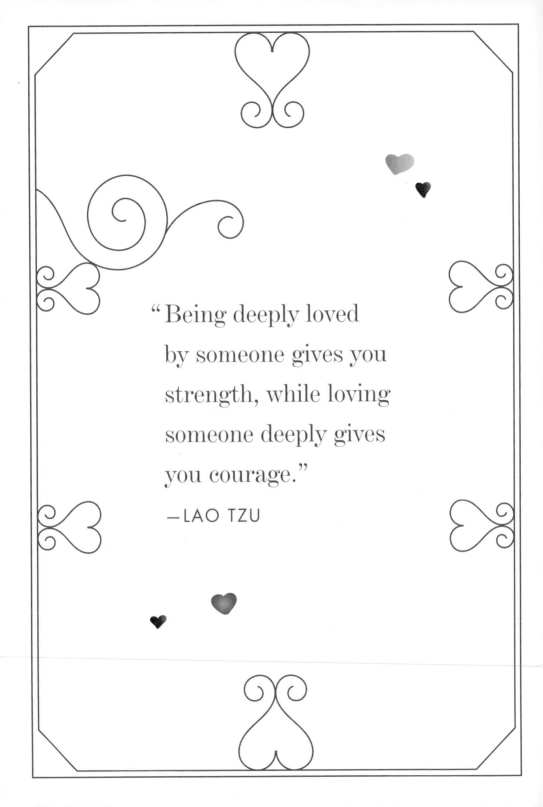

"Being deeply loved
by someone gives you
strength, while loving
someone deeply gives
you courage."

—LAO TZU

ABOUT US

Our love grows with

every moment and

deepens with every

obstacle we overcome.

Together, our love

conquers all. It's not about

you or me, it's about us.

AS A COUPLE, WE'RE BEST AT . . .

....
....
....
....
....
....
....
....
....
....
....
....

AS A COUPLE, WE'RE STILL WORKING ON . . .

....
....
....
....
....
....
....
....
....
....
....
....
....
....

AS A COUPLE, WE'RE BEST AT . . .

....
....
....
....
....
....
....
....
....
....
....
....
....

AS A COUPLE, WE'RE STILL WORKING ON . . .

....
....
....
....
....
....
....
....
....
....
....
....
....
....
....

THE BIGGEST MISTAKE I LEARNED FROM WAS . . .

....
....
....
....
....
....
....
....
....
....
....
....

I LEARNED HOW IMPORTANT SORRY WAS WHEN . . .

....
....
....
....
....
....
....
....
....
....
....
....
....
....
....
....

THE BIGGEST MISTAKE I LEARNED FROM WAS . . .

....
....
....
....
....
....
....
....
....
....
....

I LEARNED HOW IMPORTANT SORRY WAS WHEN . . .

....
....
....
....
....
....
....
....
....
....
....
....
....
....
....

A HABIT OF MINE THAT DRIVES YOU CRAZY IS . . .

....
....
....
....
....
....
....
....
....
....
....

THE WAY TO MAKE YOU LAUGH IS . . .

....
....
....
....
....
....
....
....
....
....
....
....
....
....

A HABIT OF MINE THAT DRIVES YOU CRAZY IS . . .

....
....
....
....
....
....
....
....
....
....
....
....

THE WAY TO MAKE YOU LAUGH IS . . .

....
....
....
....
....
....
....
....
....
....
....
....
....
....

THE BEST WAY TO SAY SORRY IS . . .

....

....

....

....

....

....

....

....

....

....

....

THE BEST WAY I KNOW TO KEEP YOU HAPPY IS . . .

....

....

....

....

....

....

....

....

....

....

....

....

....

THE BEST WAY TO SAY SORRY IS . . .

....

....

....

....

....

....

....

....

....

....

....

....

THE BEST WAY I KNOW TO KEEP YOU HAPPY IS . . .

....

....

....

....

....

....

....

....

....

....

....

....

....

....

MY LOVE LETTER TO: _____

MY LOVE LETTER TO: _____

THE ACTIVITY THAT WILL ALWAYS CHEER YOU UP IS . . .

....
....
....
....
....

THE FOOD THAT WILL ALWAYS BRING YOU COMFORT IS . . .

....
....
....
....
....
....

THE THING THAT WILL ALWAYS MAKE YOU SMILE . . .

....
....
....
....
....
....
....
....

THE ACTIVITY THAT WILL ALWAYS CHEER YOU UP IS . . .

....

....

....

....

....

THE FOOD THAT WILL ALWAYS BRING YOU COMFORT IS . . .

....

....

....

....

....

....

THE THING THAT WILL ALWAYS MAKE YOU SMILE . . .

....

....

....

....

....

....

....

I FELT THE MOST LOVED WHEN . . .

....

....

....

....

....

....

....

....

....

....

....

....

....

....

....

....

....

....

....

....

....

....

....

....

....

....

....

....

I FELT THE MOST LOVED WHEN . . .

THE WAYS IN WHICH I HOPE TO GROW . . .

....

....

....

....

....

....

....

....

....

....

....

....

....

....

....

....

....

....

....

....

....

....

....

THE WAYS IN WHICH I HOPE TO GROW . . .

....

....

....

....

....

....

....

....

....

....

....

....

....

....

....

....

....

....

....

....

....

....

....

....

....

....

....

....

....

♥

THE PERFECT FIT Relationships are never perfect. But they feel that way when we take the time to stop, listen, and care. Our relationship works because we know each other. We know each other's hopes and fears as well as each other's strengths and weaknesses. Show your partner how much you care by completing the partner map:

THE QUALITIES ABOUT YOU THAT MADE ME FALL IN LOVE . . .
1.
2.
3.

THINGS YOU DO I CAN'T LIVE WITHOUT:
1.
2.
3.

YOUR BIGGEST FEARS ARE:
1.
2.
3.

YOU'RE HAPPIEST WHEN:
1.
2.
3.

THE MOST IMPORTANT THINGS TO YOU IN LIFE (BESIDES US) ARE:
1.
2.
3.

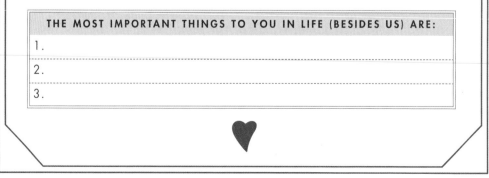

THE PERFECT FIT Relationships are never perfect. But they feel that way when we take the time to stop, listen, and care. Our relationship works because we know each other. We know each other's hopes and fears as well as each other's strengths and weaknesses. Show your partner how much you care by completing the partner map:

THE QUALITIES ABOUT YOU THAT MADE ME FALL IN LOVE . . .

1.
2.
3.

THINGS YOU DO I CAN'T LIVE WITHOUT:

1.
2.
3.

YOUR BIGGEST FEARS ARE:

1.
2.
3.

YOU'RE HAPPIEST WHEN:

1.
2.
3.

THE MOST IMPORTANT THINGS TO YOU IN LIFE (BESIDES US) ARE:

1.
2.
3.

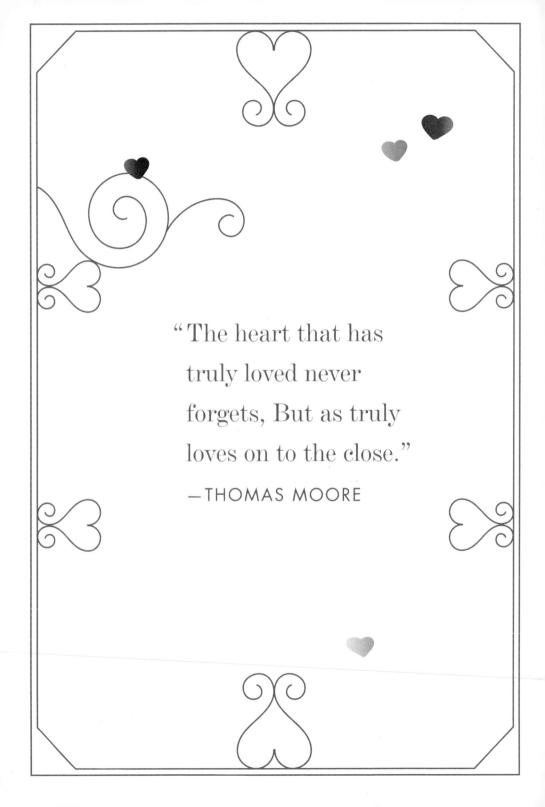

"The heart that has truly loved never forgets, But as truly loves on to the close."

—THOMAS MOORE

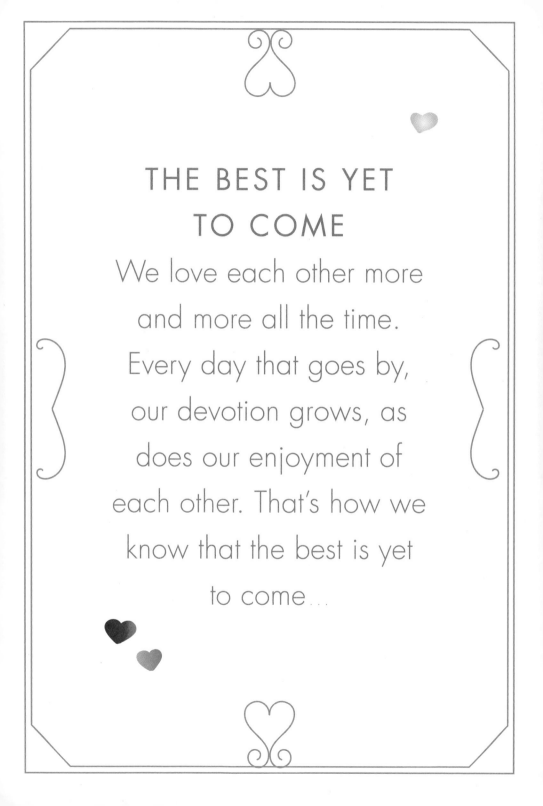

THE BEST IS YET TO COME

We love each other more
and more all the time.
Every day that goes by,
our devotion grows, as
does our enjoyment of
each other. That's how we
know that the best is yet
to come...

I CAN'T WAIT TO DO THIS WITH YOU . . .

I CAN'T WAIT TO DO THIS WITH YOU . . .

OUR NEXT BIG ADVENTURE WILL BE . . .

....
....
....
....
....
....
....
....
....
....
....
....
....

IF WE COULD GO ANYWHERE IN THE WORLD, WE'D . . .

....
....
....
....
....
....
....
....
....
....
....
....
....
....
....
....

OUR NEXT BIG ADVENTURE WILL BE . . .

IF WE COULD GO ANYWHERE IN THE WORLD, WE'D . . .

IF WE WON THE LOTTERY TOMORROW, WE'D . . .

....
....
....
....
....
....
....
....
....
....
....
....

WE CAN'T WAIT UNTIL WE . . .

....
....
....
....
....
....
....
....
....
....
....
....
....

♥

IF WE WON THE LOTTERY TOMORROW, WE'D . . .

....

....

....

....

....

....

....

....

....

....

....

....

WE CAN'T WAIT UNTIL WE . . .

....

....

....

....

....

....

....

....

....

....

....

....

....

....

....

OUR BUCKET LIST

THERE IS SO MUCH WE CAN'T WAIT TO DO TOGETHER!

PLACES TO GO:

1 ....
2 ....
3 ....
4 ....
5 ....
6 ....
7 ....
8 ....
9 ....
10 ....

THINGS TO LEARN:

1 ....
2 ....
3 ....
4 ....
5 ....
6 ....
7 ....
8 ....
9 ....
10 ....

OUR BUCKET LIST

THERE IS SO MUCH WE CAN'T WAIT TO DO TOGETHER!

PLACES TO GO:

1 ....
2 ....
3 ....
4 ....
5 ....
6 ....
7 ....
8 ....
9 ....
10 ....

THINGS TO LEARN:

1 ....
2 ....
3 ....
4 ....
5 ....
6 ....
7 ....
8 ....
9 ....
10 ....

THE NEXT TIME WE ARGUE, INSTEAD OF DOING WHAT I USUALLY DO, I'LL . . .

THE NEXT TIME WE ARGUE, INSTEAD OF DOING WHAT I USUALLY DO, I'LL . . .

THE NEXT MEMORY I WANT WITH YOU IS . . .

....
....
....
....
....
....
....
....
....
....
....
....

I LOVE SPENDING TIME WITH YOU BECAUSE . . .

....
....
....
....
....
....
....
....
....
....
....
....
....
....

♥

THE NEXT MEMORY I WANT WITH YOU IS . . .

....

....

....

....

....

....

....

....

....

....

....

I LOVE SPENDING TIME WITH YOU BECAUSE . . .

....

....

....

....

....

....

....

....

....

....

....

....

....

....

....

THE NEXT THING WE WILL DO FOR OUR HOME WILL BE . . .

THE NEXT THING WE WILL CREATE TOGETHER WILL BE . . .

WE'VE ALWAYS TALKED ABOUT DOING THIS, SO LET'S . . .

FOR OUR NEXT ANNIVERSARY, LET'S . . .

TO THE FUTURE US

HERE ARE SOME WORDS OF ADVICE, HOPES,
AND MEMORIES WE WILL ALWAYS TREASURE.

WE HOPE WE ALWAYS . . .

LET'S NEVER FORGET . . .

LET'S ALWAYS REMEMBER TO . . .

OUR BEST ADVICE FOR FUTURE US:

OUR FAVORITE MEMORY SO FAR:

OUR FONDEST WISH FOR THE FUTURE:

THE MISTAKE WE CAN'T EVER REPEAT:

THE TIP THAT'LL ALWAYS MAKE THINGS BETTER:

THE THING THAT'LL ALWAYS MAKE YOU SMILE:

THE LESSON THAT'LL GET US THROUGH ANY PROBLEM:

THE WORDS I'LL NEVER FORGET TO SAY:

THE THING I'LL NEVER FORGET TO DO:

THE MEMORY THAT I WILL ALWAYS HOLD DEAR:

THE WAY WE FEEL RIGHT AT THIS MOMENT:

WE CAN OVERCOME ANY OBSTACLE IF WE REMEMBER . . .

A TRADITION I WOULD LIKE TO BEGIN WITH YOU IS . . .

....

....

....

....

....

....

....

....

....

....

....

....

I COULDN'T IMAGINE A BETTER PARTNER IN . . .

....

....

....

....

....

....

....

....

....

....

....

....

....

A TRADITION I WOULD LIKE TO BEGIN WITH YOU IS . . .

....

....

....

....

....

....

....

....

....

....

....

I COULDN'T IMAGINE A BETTER PARTNER IN . . .

....

....

....

....

....

....

....

....

....

....

....

....

WE'RE THE BEST TEAM BECAUSE . . .

....

....

....

....

....

....

....

....

....

....

....

I'LL ALWAYS NEED YOU . . .

....

....

....

....

....

....

....

....

....

....

....

....

....

♥

WE'RE THE BEST TEAM BECAUSE . . .

....
....
....
....
....
....
....
....
....
....
....
....

I'LL ALWAYS NEED YOU . . .

....
....
....
....
....
....
....
....
....
....
....
....
....
....

IN FIVE YEARS, I THINK WE'LL . . .

....
....
....
....
....
....
....
....
....
....
....
....

IN TWENTY YEARS, I THINK WE'LL . . .

....
....
....
....
....
....
....
....
....
....
....
....
....
....

IN FIVE YEARS, I THINK WE'LL . . .

....
....
....
....
....
....
....
....
....
....
....

IN TWENTY YEARS, I THINK WE'LL . . .

....
....
....
....
....
....
....
....
....
....
....
....
....
....

♥

WHEN I THINK ABOUT WHAT YOU'LL BE LIKE IN THE FUTURE, I IMAGINE . . .

WHEN I THINK ABOUT WHAT YOU'LL BE LIKE IN THE FUTURE, I IMAGINE . . .

I HOPE OUR LIFE TOGETHER IN THE FUTURE WILL . . .

I HOPE OUR LIFE TOGETHER IN THE FUTURE WILL . . .

A MILLION REASONS WHY

THERE ARE A MILLION REASONS WHY I LOVE YOU,
AND HERE'S A LIST FROM A TO Z.

I LOVE YOU BECAUSE YOU . . .

A	N
B	O
C	P
D	Q
E	R
F	S
G	T
H	U
I	V
J	W
K	X
L	Y
M	Z

Inspiring | Educating | Creating | Entertaining

Brimming with creative inspiration, how-to projects, and useful information to enrich your everyday life, quarto.com is a favorite destination for those pursuing their interests and passions.

© 2021 by Quarto Publishing Group USA Inc.

This edition published in 2022 by Chartwell Books,
an imprint of The Quarto Group,
142 West 36th Street, 4th Floor,
New York, NY 10018, USA
T (212) 779-4972 f (212) 779-6058
www.Quarto.com

Previously published in 2021 by Chartwell Books, an imprint of The Quarto Group,
142 West 36th Street, 4th Floor, New York, NY 10018, USA

Chartwell titles are also available at discount for retail, wholesale, promotional, and bulk purchase. For details, contact the special sales manager by email at specialsales@quarto.com or by mail at The Quarto Group, ATTN: Special Sales Manager, 100 Cummings Center, Suite 265D, Beverly, MA 01915, USA.

10 9 8 7 6 5 4 3 2

ISBN: 978-0-7858-4039-8

Publisher: Rage Kindelsperger
Creative Director: Laura Drew
Managing Editor: Cara Donaldson
Project Editor: Leeann Moreau
Text: Sarosh Arif
Cover Design: Beth Middleworth
Interior Design: Beth Middleworth

Printed in China

A MILLION REASONS WHY

THERE ARE A MILLION REASONS WHY I LOVE YOU,
AND HERE'S A LIST FROM A TO Z.

I LOVE YOU BECAUSE YOU . . .

A		N	
B		O	
C		P	
D		Q	
E		R	
F		S	
G		T	
H		U	
I		V	
J		W	
K		X	
L		Y	
M		Z	